EARLY CIVILIZATIONS OF THE AMERICAS

Contents

These are dangerous animals.
Look at the huge tusks on the mammoth.
Do these tigers look like tigers today?

Early people hunted animals.
They used animal fur, skin, and bones.
How did these people use animal skins?

People learned how to grow corn.
Then they could live in one place.
They did not have to wander to look for food.

People built these houses long ago.
They could live in villages like this one.

Maya artists carved this statue out of stone.
It guards a stairway to a temple.

Buildings like this are called pyramids.
The Maya built many pyramids.
Some were temples, and some were palaces.

These tools helped the Maya to count things.
Maya numbers used lines, circles or dots, and ovals.
A line is 5, a dot is 1, and an oval is zero.

The Aztec market was a busy place.
People brought food, pots, and crafts to trade.
Can you find these things in the picture?

A god told the Aztecs to look for a lake,
an eagle, a snake, and a cactus.
That is where they would build a great city.

The Aztecs built bridges from their island to the shore of the lake.
They built canals, or waterways, on the island.

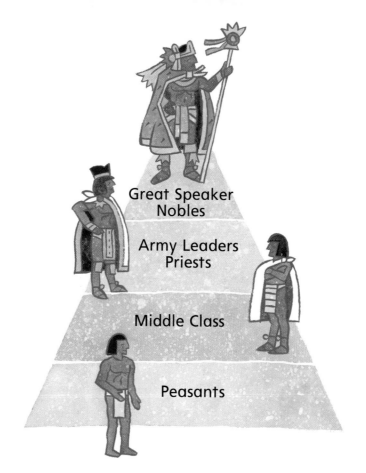

Great Speaker
Nobles

Army Leaders
Priests

Middle Class

Peasants

The Great Speaker and the nobles were the
most important Aztecs.
Who was next?

It was easy to travel through the mountains
if you were carried in a chair.
How did the queen cross the river?

The Incas built this city out of heavy blocks of stone. No one really knows how they were able to move the stones to build high walls.

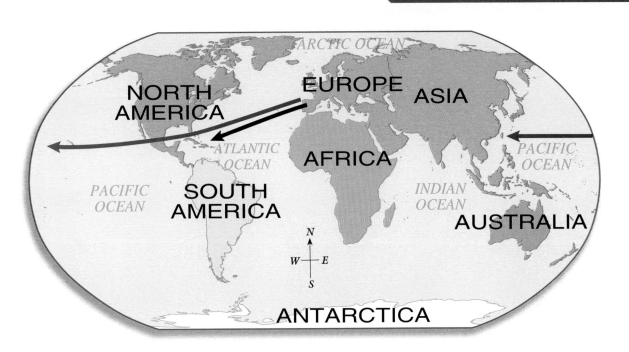

Christopher Columbus wanted to sail to Asia.
The red line shows his plan.
The black line shows what really happened.

The king and queen of Spain helped Columbus.
They gave him three ships to carry out his plan.
They hoped he would sail to the Indies.

Columbus thought he had landed in the Indies. He was so sure of it that he called the people who greeted him Indians.

Christopher Columbus always believed that
he had reached Asia.
He made three more trips to look for riches.

Cortés heard about the rich city of the Aztecs. He wanted the gold, silver, and jewels that were there.

The Aztec ruler sent Cortés presents like this one.
He hoped that Cortés would take these treasures
and go away.

Montezuma welcomed Cortés to his city.
Cortés was not friendly.
He made Montezuma a prisoner.

Pizarro wanted to find Inca gold and treasure.
Many of his men were afraid to follow him.
Some men crossed the line he drew in the sand.

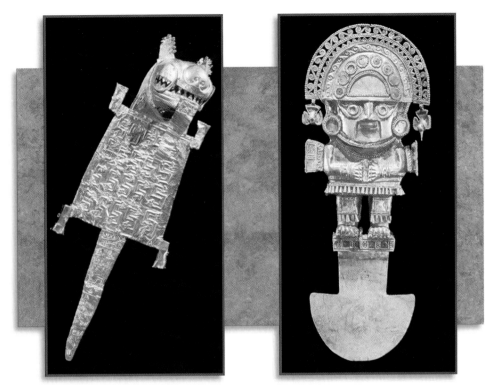

Gold jewelry

Pizarro captured the Grand Inca.
Pizarro told the Incas to fill a room with gold
to save their leader.

Pizarro tricked the Incas.
He took the gold but did not free the Grand Inca.
Then Pizarro killed the Grand Inca.